GINGERBREAD SNOWMAN ORNAMENT

Photo, pg. 5

Please read General Instructions, pg. 1.

SUPPLIES

Heavyweight brown paper bag
Acrylic paints — light ivory, black, red, and orange
Antiquing medium or burnt umber acrylic paint
Paintbrushes
White dimensional paint
Polyester fiberfill
19-gauge annealed wire
$1/2$" dia. wooden dowel
Clear acrylic spray sealer
Trims — fabrics, jingle bell, raffia, and a button
General Supplies — toothbrush, pliers, wire cutters,
   tracing paper, graphite paper, scissors, and a hot glue
   gun and glue sticks

INSTRUCTIONS

1. Transfer and cut out two Gingerbread Snowman pieces (pg. 12) from brown paper bag.
2. Paint one Gingerbread Snowman piece.
3. Antique Gingerbread Snowman.
4. Spatter paint Gingerbread Snowman with light ivory acrylic paint.
5. Spray project with acrylic sealer.
6. Apply white dimensional paint for icing trim; allow to dry.
7. Leaving an opening for stuffing, glue edges of Gingerbread Snowman pieces together; stuff with small pieces of fiberfill and glue closed.
8. Cut a 34" length of wire. Add wire hanger to Gingerbread Snowman.
9. Add trims to Gingerbread Snowman as follows:
     Glue fabric quick-knot bow and jingle bell to Gingerbread Snowman.
     Glue raffia shoelace-style bow, fabric quick-knot bow, and button to hanger.

GINGERBREAD BOY ORNAMENT

Photo, front cover

Please read General Instructions, pg. 1.

SUPPLIES

Heavyweight brown paper bag
Acrylic paints — light brown, black, red, and light ivory
Paintbrushes
White dimensional paint
Polyester fiberfill
19-gauge annealed wire
$1/2$" dia. wooden dowel
Clear acrylic spray sealer
Black fine-point permanent pen
Trims — fabrics, jingle bell, raffia, and a button
General Supplies — toothbrush, pliers, wire cutters,
   tracing paper, graphite paper, scissors, and a hot glue
   gun and glue sticks

INSTRUCTIONS

1. Transfer and cut out two Gingerbread Boy pieces (pg. 11) from brown paper bag.
2. Paint one Gingerbread Boy piece.
3. Use permanent pen to add details to cheeks.
4. Spatter paint Gingerbread Boy with light ivory acrylic paint.
5. Spray project with acrylic sealer.
6. Apply white dimensional paint for icing trim; allow to dry.
7. Leaving an opening for stuffing, glue edges of Gingerbread Boy pieces together; stuff with small pieces of fiberfill and glue closed.
8. Cut a 34" length of wire. Add wire hanger to Gingerbread Boy.
9. Add trims to Gingerbread Boy as follows:
     Glue fabric quick-knot bow and jingle bell to Gingerbread Boy.
     Glue raffia shoelace-style bow, fabric quick-knot bow, and button to hanger.

GINGERBREAD BOY AND HEARTS GARLAND
Photo, pg. 5

Please read General Instructions, pg. 1.

SUPPLIES
Heavyweight brown paper bag
Acrylic paints — light brown, black, red, and light ivory
Paintbrushes
White dimensional paint
Polyester fiberfill
19-gauge annealed wire
Clear acrylic spray sealer
Black fine-point permanent pen
Trims — fabrics, jingle bell, and buttons
General Supplies — toothbrush, pliers, wire cutters, tracing paper, graphite paper, scissors, and a hot glue gun and glue sticks

INSTRUCTIONS
1. Transfer and cut out two Gingerbread Boy pieces and four Large Heart pieces (pg. 11) from brown paper bag.
2. Follow Steps 2-7 of Gingerbread Boy Ornament (pg. 2) to complete Gingerbread Boy and two Hearts.

3. Use wire cutters to cut two 6" pieces of wire and two 5" pieces of wire. Use one end of wire to make holes in each side of heart and in each hand of Gingerbread Boy. Insert ends of 6" pieces into holes in Gingerbread Boy hands and Hearts *(Fig. 1)*; use pliers to twist ends around wire to secure. Insert ends of 5" pieces into holes in hearts. Form a loop at each end of garland; twist ends around wire to secure *(Fig. 1)*. Trim wire ends if necessary.

Fig. 1

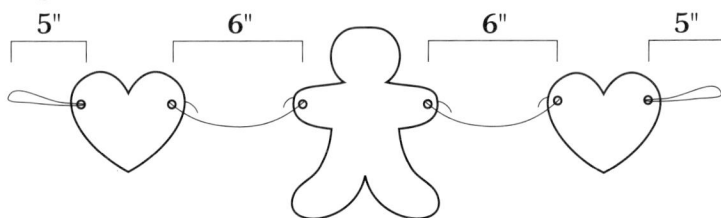

4. Add trims to garland as follows:
   Tie fabric quick-knot bows to wires between pieces and at ends of garland.
   Glue fabric quick-knot bow and jingle bell to Gingerbread Boy.
   Glue fabric patches and buttons to Hearts.

TREE ORNAMENT
Photo, pg. 5

Please read General Instructions, pg. 1.

SUPPLIES
Heavyweight brown paper bag
Acrylic paints — green and light ivory
Paintbrushes
Polyester fiberfill
19-gauge annealed wire
$1/2$" dia. wooden dowel
Clear acrylic spray sealer
Trims — buttons, raffia, fabric, cinnamon stick, and a jingle bell
General Supplies — toothbrush, pliers, wire cutters, tracing paper, graphite paper, scissors, and a hot glue gun and glue sticks

INSTRUCTIONS
1. Transfer and cut out two Tree pieces (pg. 24) from brown paper bag.
2. Paint one Tree piece.
3. Spatter paint Tree with light ivory acrylic paint.
4. Spray project with acrylic sealer.
5. Leaving an opening at bottom for stuffing, glue Tree pieces together; stuff with small pieces of fiberfill. Insert cinnamon stick in opening and glue closed around stick.
6. Cut a 27" length of wire. Add wire hanger to Tree.
7. Add trims to Tree as follows:
   Glue buttons to Tree.
   Glue raffia shoelace-style bow, fabric quick-knot bow, and jingle bell to hanger.

SQUARE SANTA BOX
Photo, pg. 6

Please read General Instructions, pg. 1.

SUPPLIES
Papier-mâché box with 5¼" square lid
Acrylic paints — flesh, red, light ivory, and black
Antiquing medium or burnt umber acrylic paint
DecoArt® Snow-Tex™
Paintbrushes
Palette knife
Clear acrylic spray sealer
Trims — fabrics and a button
General Supplies — toothbrush, tracing paper, graphite paper, and a hot glue gun and glue sticks

INSTRUCTIONS
1. Draw a line diagonally across box lid from corner to corner.
2. Paint one half of lid red; paint remaining half light ivory. Paint box bottom red.
3. Trace Square Santa Box Face pattern (pg. 8) onto tracing paper. Place graphite paper, coated side down, on box lid. Place traced pattern on top of graphite paper with top of face along painted line. Draw over traced pattern.
4. Paint face.
5. Antique beard portion of box lid.
6. Covering beard portion with a scrap of brown paper, spatter paint box lid and box bottom with light ivory acrylic paint.
7. Texturize hat trim using Snow-Tex.
8. Spray project with acrylic sealer.
9. Glue fabric patches and button to box lid.

ROUND SANTA BOX
Photo, pg. 6

Please read General Instructions, pg. 1.

SUPPLIES
Papier-mâché box with 6¼" dia. lid
Acrylic paints — flesh, red, light ivory, green, and black
Antiquing medium or burnt umber acrylic paint
Liquitex® Texture Gel Light Modeling Paste
Paintbrushes
Palette knife
Clear acrylic spray sealer
Iridescent glitter
Black fine-point permanent pen
Trims — buttons
General Supplies — toothbrush, tracing paper, graphite paper, craft glue, and a hot glue gun and glue sticks

INSTRUCTIONS
1. Paint ⅓ of box lid red; paint remaining ⅔ light ivory. Paint box bottom red.
2. Trace Round Santa Box Face pattern (pg. 8) onto tracing paper. Place graphite paper, coated side down, on box lid. Place traced pattern on top of graphite paper with top of face along painted line. Draw over traced pattern.
3. Paint face and add stripes and dots to box lid.
4. Use permanent pen to add details to patches and around box lid.
5. Texturize hat trim and mustache using Modeling Paste.
6. Antique hat trim and mustache.
7. Spatter paint box lid with light ivory acrylic paint.
8. Spray project with acrylic sealer.
9. Spread a thin layer of craft glue over box lid and bottom. Sprinkle on glitter; shake off excess.
10. Hot glue buttons to box lid.

4

5

SQUARE SANTA ORNAMENTS

Photo, back cover

Please read General Instructions, pg. 1.

SUPPLIES

Heavyweight brown paper bag
Acrylic paints — flesh, red, light ivory, and black
Antiquing medium or burnt umber acrylic paint
DecoArt® Snow-Tex™
Paintbrushes
Palette knife
Polyester fiberfill
Clear acrylic spray sealer
Jute
Trims — fabrics and a button
General Supplies — toothbrush, tracing paper, graphite paper, scissors, and a hot glue gun and glue sticks

INSTRUCTIONS

1. For each ornament, transfer and cut out two Square Santa Ornament pieces (pg. 8) from brown paper bag.
2. Paint one Square Santa piece.
3. Antique beard portion.
4. Covering beard portion with a scrap of brown paper, spatter paint hat portion with light ivory acrylic paint.
5. Texturize hat trim using Snow-Tex.
6. Spray project with acrylic sealer.
7. Leaving an opening for stuffing, glue Square Santa pieces together; stuff with small pieces of fiberfill and glue closed.
8. Cut a 5" length of jute. Glue ends of jute to back of Square Santa.
9. Glue fabric patches and button to Santa.

SANTA POCKET ORNAMENTS

Photos, front and back covers

Please read General Instructions, pg. 1.

SUPPLIES

Heavyweight brown paper bag
Acrylic paints — flesh, light ivory, black, red, and green
Paintbrushes
19-gauge annealed wire
1/2" dia. wooden dowel
Clear acrylic spray sealer
Black fine-point permanent pen
Trims — raffia, jingle bell, artificial greenery, artificial pinecones, artificial berries, and fabrics
General Supplies — toothbrush, pliers, wire cutters, tracing paper, graphite paper, scissors, and a hot glue gun and glue sticks

INSTRUCTIONS

1. For each ornament, transfer and cut out two pattern pieces (pgs. 11 and 12) from brown paper bag.
2. Paint one piece.
3. Use permanent pen to add details.
4. Spatter paint piece with black acrylic paint.
5. Spray project with acrylic sealer.
6. Leaving an opening at top, glue pieces together.
7. Cut an 18" length of wire. Add wire hanger to project.
8. Add trims to project as follows:
    Glue raffia shoelace-style bow and jingle bell to hanger.
    Glue artificial greenery, pinecones, and berries in opening.
    Glue fabric patches to project.

Square Santa Ornament

Round Santa Box Face

Square Santa Box Face

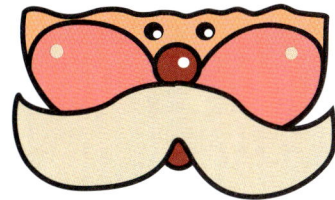

Santa Stocking Face
Santa Bag Face

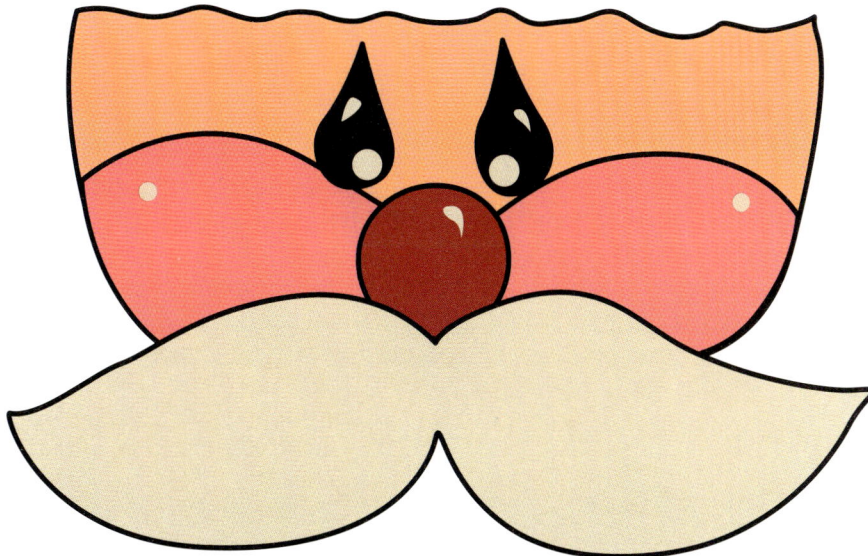

SANTA STOCKING
Photo, pg. 15

Please read General Instructions, pg. 1.

SUPPLIES
Heavyweight brown paper bag
Acrylic paints — red, light ivory, flesh, and black
Antiquing medium or burnt umber acrylic paint
Liquitex® Texture Gel Light Modeling Paste
Paintbrushes
Palette knife
19-gauge annealed wire
1/2" dia. wooden dowel
Clear acrylic spray sealer
Trims — raffia, jingle bell, fabrics, and a button
General Supplies — toothbrush, pliers, wire cutters, tracing paper, graphite paper, scissors, and a hot glue gun and glue sticks

INSTRUCTIONS
1. Transfer and cut out two Large Stocking pieces (pgs. 27-28) from brown paper bag.
2. For cuff, paint 3" below top edge of Stocking red; paint remaining Stocking light ivory.
3. Trace Santa Stocking Face pattern (pg. 8) onto tracing paper. Place graphite paper, coated side down, on Stocking front. Place traced pattern on top of graphite paper. Draw over traced pattern.
4. Paint face.
5. Texturize hat trim and mustache using Modeling Paste.
6. Antique Stocking.
7. Spatter paint Stocking with light ivory acrylic paint.
8. Spray project with acrylic sealer.
9. Leaving an opening at top, glue Stocking pieces together.
10. Cut a 39" length of wire. Add wire hanger to Stocking.
11. Add trims to Stocking as follows:
    Glue raffia shoelace-style bows and jingle bell to hanger.
    Glue fabric patches and button to Stocking.

ANGEL STOCKING
Photo, front cover

Please read General Instructions, pg. 1.

SUPPLIES
Heavyweight brown paper bag
Acrylic paints — red, light ivory, flesh, and black
Paintbrushes
Paper-backed fusible web
19-gauge annealed wire
1/2" dia. wooden dowel
Clear acrylic spray sealer
Black fine-point permanent pen
Trims — raffia, buttons, fabrics, excelsior, and a jingle bell
General Supplies — toothbrush, pliers, wire cutters, tracing paper, graphite paper, scissors, and a hot glue gun and glue sticks

INSTRUCTIONS
1. Transfer and cut out two Large Stocking pieces (pgs. 27-28) and one Angel Stocking Body piece (pg. 19) from brown paper bag.
2. Trace Angel Stocking Wings pattern (pg. 20) onto paper-backing side of fusible web. Fuse web to wrong side of fabric; cut along drawn line.
3. Paint Angel Stocking Body piece.
4. Use permanent pen to add details to cheeks and feet.
5. Spray Angel Stocking Body with acrylic sealer.
6. Fuse Angel Stocking Wings to Large Stocking; glue Angel Stocking Body to Large Stocking.
7. Use permanent pen to add details to edge of stocking.
8. Leaving an opening at top, glue Stocking pieces together.
9. Spatter paint Stocking with light ivory acrylic paint.
10. Cut a 39" length of wire. Add wire hanger to Stocking.
11. Add trims to Stocking as follows:
    Glue raffia shoelace-style bows and button to hanger.
    Glue fabric patches, raffia shoelace-style bow, excelsior, buttons, and jingle bell to Stocking.

PAPER BAG STOCKINGS

Photos, front cover and pg. 15

Please read General Instructions, pg. 1.

SUPPLIES

Heavyweight brown paper bag
Light ivory acrylic paint
White dimensional paint
19-gauge annealed wire
$1/2$" dia. wooden dowel
Trims — raffia, fabrics, buttons, and a jingle bell
General Supplies — toothbrush, pliers, wire cutters, tracing paper, graphite paper, scissors, and a hot glue gun and glue sticks

For Fabric Heart stocking, you will also need:
Paper-backed fusible web

For Gingerbread Boy stocking, you will also need:
Acrylic paints — dark brown, red, and black
Compressed craft sponges
Paper plate
Paper towels
Fine-point permanent pen

For Holly stocking, you will also need:
Acrylic paints — green and red
Compressed craft sponges
Paper plate
Paper towels
Fine-point permanent pen

For Stars stocking, you will also need:
Acrylic paint — gold
Compressed craft sponges
Paper plate
Paper towels
Fine-point permanent pen

INSTRUCTIONS

1. For each stocking, transfer and cut out two Stocking pieces (pgs. 27-29) of desired size from brown paper bag.
2. **For Fabric Heart stocking,** trace Medium Heart pattern (pg. 24) desired number of times onto paper-backing side of fusible web. Fuse web to wrong side of fabrics; cut along drawn lines. Fuse hearts to one Stocking piece.
3. **For remaining stockings**, sponge paint shapes (pg. 24) desired number of times on Stocking. **For Holly stocking**, add berries with acrylic paint and the eraser end of a pencil. **For Gingerbread Boy stocking**, add eyes, buttons, and bows with acrylic paints.
4. Spatter paint Stocking with light ivory acrylic paint.
5. Apply white dimensional paint for icing; allow to dry.
6. Leaving an opening at top, glue Stocking pieces together.
7. **For large stocking**, cut a 39" length of wire. **For medium stocking**, cut a 34" length of wire. Add wire hanger to Stocking.
8. Add trims to Stockings as follows:
   Glue raffia shoelace-style bow, fabric quick-knot bow, and button to hanger.
   Glue fabric patches, buttons, and jingle bell to stocking.

Large Heart

Santa Pocket

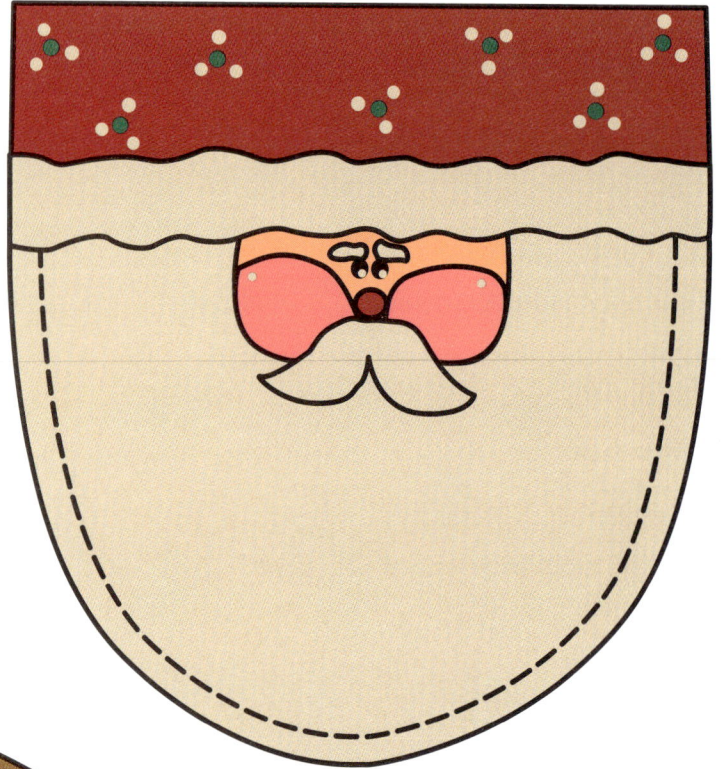

Gingerbread Boy

11

Heart Santa Pocket

Stocking Santa Pocket

Gingerbread Snowman

FABRIC PATCH STOCKINGS

Photos, front cover, back cover, and pg. 15

Please read General Instructions, pg. 1.

SUPPLIES

Heavyweight brown paper bag
Acrylic paints — red, green, or light ivory
Paintbrushes
19-gauge annealed wire
1/2" dia. wooden dowel (for medium or large stocking
 only)
Clear acrylic spray sealer
Trims — raffia, buttons, fabrics, and jingle bells
General Supplies — pliers, wire cutters, tracing paper,
 graphite paper, scissors, and a hot glue gun and glue
 sticks

For ivory stocking, you will also need:
Antiquing medium or burnt umber acrylic paint

For red or green stocking, you will also need:
Toothbrush

INSTRUCTIONS

1. For each stocking, transfer and cut out two Stocking pieces (pgs. 27-29) of desired size from brown paper bag.
2. Paint one Stocking piece.
3. **For ivory stocking**, antique Stocking. **For red or green stocking**, spatter paint with light ivory acrylic paint.
4. Spray project with acrylic sealer.
5. Leaving an opening at top, glue Stocking pieces together.
6. **For large stocking**, cut a 39" length of wire. Add wire hanger to Stocking. **For medium stocking**, cut a 34" length of wire. Add wire hanger to Stocking. **For small stocking**, cut a 7" length of wire. Add wire hanger to Stocking without curling wire around dowel.
7. Add trims to Stocking as follows:
   Glue raffia shoelace-style bow and button to Stocking.
   Glue fabric patches, buttons, and jingle bell to Stocking.

TREETOP ANGEL

Photo, back cover

Please read General Instructions, pg. 1.

SUPPLIES

Heavyweight brown paper bag
Acrylic paints — flesh, red, green, light ivory, and black
Antiquing medium or burnt umber acrylic paint
Paintbrushes
Black fine-point permanent pen
Paper-backed fusible web
Polyester fiberfill
Clear acrylic spray sealer
Pressing cloth
Trims — excelsior, 2" dia. grapevine wreath, raffia,
 jingle bell, fabrics, and buttons
General Supplies — toothbrush, tracing paper, graphite
 paper, scissors, and a hot glue gun and glue sticks

INSTRUCTIONS

1. Transfer and cut out two Treetop Angel Body pieces (pg. 23) and two Treetop Angel Wing pieces (pg. 20) from brown paper bag.
2. Paint one Treetop Angel Body and one Treetop Angel Wing piece.
3. Use permanent pen to add details to cheeks and dress.
4. Antique Treetop Angel Body and Treetop Angel Wing pieces.
5. Spatter paint Treetop Angel Body with light ivory acrylic paint.
6. Spray Treetop Angel Body and Treetop Angel Wing with acrylic sealer.
7. Trace Treetop Angel Wing pattern onto paper backing side of fusible web. Fuse web to wrong side of fabric; cut 1/4" inside drawn line. Using pressing cloth, center and fuse fabric wing to painted wing piece.
8. Leaving an opening for stuffing, glue Treetop Angel Wing pieces together; stuff with small pieces of fiberfill and glue closed. Leaving an opening at bottom, glue Treetop Angel Body pieces together; stuff head with small pieces of fiberfill.
9. Glue Treetop Angel Wing to back of Treetop Angel Body.
10. Glue excelsior, grapevine wreath, raffia shoelace-style bow, jingle bell, fabric patches, and buttons to Angel.

13

NAPKIN TIES

Photo, pg. 5

Please read General Instructions, pg. 1.

SUPPLIES

Corrugated cardboard
Paper-backed fusible web
Fabric
Jute
Trims — buttons
General Supplies — tracing paper, craft knife, scissors, and a hot glue gun and glue sticks

INSTRUCTIONS

1. For each napkin tie, trace Medium Heart or Holly pattern (pg. 24) onto tracing paper; cut out. Draw around pattern on corrugated cardboard; cut out.
2. Trace Medium Heart or Holly pattern onto paper-backing side of fusible web. Fuse web to wrong side of fabric; cut along drawn line.
3. Fuse one fabric piece to one cardboard piece.
4. Glue a 12" length of jute to back of each napkin tie.
5. Glue buttons to napkin tie.

PLACE MATS

Photo, pg. 5

Please read General Instructions, pg. 1.

SUPPLIES

Brown kraft paper
Light ivory acrylic paint
Fusible fleece
Paper-backed fusible web
Fabrics
Decorative-edge scissors
Trims — buttons
General Supplies — toothbrush and a hot glue gun and glue sticks

INSTRUCTIONS

1. For each place mat, use decorative-edge scissors to cut an 18" x 12½" piece of kraft paper. Measuring 3¼" from each corner, make a mark. Draw a diagonal line between marks *(Fig. 1)*; trim corners with decorative-edge scissors.
2. Cut a piece of fleece slightly smaller than place mat. Fuse fleece to one side of kraft paper.
3. Spatter paint place mat using light ivory acrylic paint.
4. Trace Medium Heart or Holly pattern (pg. 24) desired number of times onto paper-backing side of fusible web. Fuse web to wrong side of fabrics; cut along drawn line.
5. Fuse shapes to place mat.
6. Glue buttons to place mat.

Fig. 1

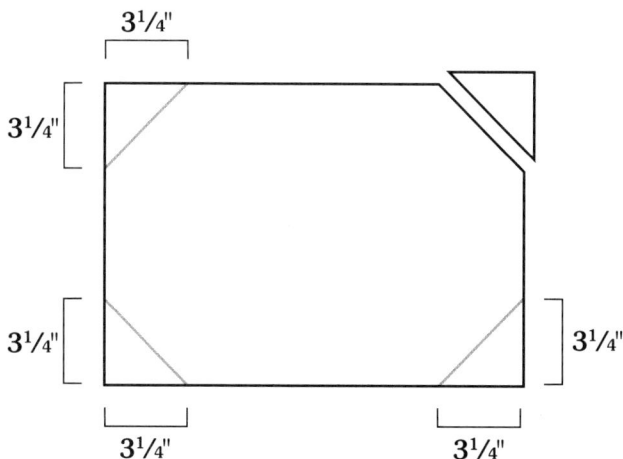

3¼"
3¼"
3¼"
3¼"
3¼"
3¼"

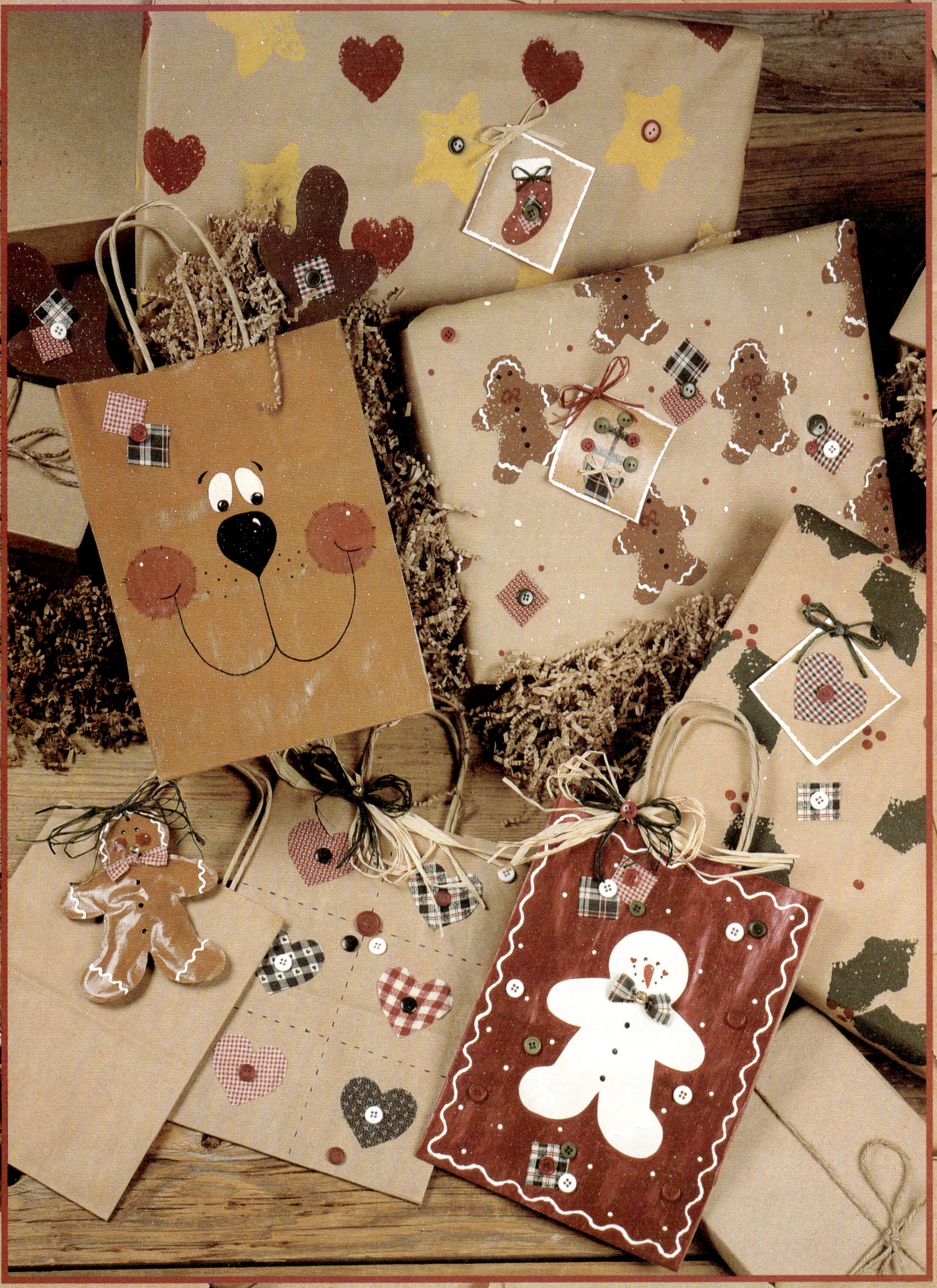

REINDEER BAG

Photo, pg. 16

Please read General Instructions, pg. 1.

SUPPLIES

8"w x 10½"h x 4½"d gift bag
Corrugated cardboard
Acrylic paints — light brown, dark brown, red, light ivory, and black
Paintbrushes
Clear acrylic spray sealer
Trims — fabrics and buttons
General Supplies — toothbrush, tracing paper, graphite paper, craft knife, and a hot glue gun and glue sticks

INSTRUCTIONS

1. Trace Reindeer Bag Antler pattern (pg. 25) onto tracing paper; cut out. Draw around pattern on corrugated cardboard; cut out.
2. Paint bag light brown; paint antlers dark brown.
3. Trace Reindeer Bag Face pattern (pg. 25) onto tracing paper. Place graphite paper, coated side down, on bag. Place traced pattern on top of graphite paper. Draw over traced pattern.
4. Paint face.
5. Glue antlers inside bag.
6. Spatter paint bag and antlers with light ivory acrylic paint.
7. Spray bag and antlers with acrylic sealer.
8. Glue fabric patches and buttons to reindeer.

SANTA BAG

Photo, front cover

Please read General Instructions, pg. 1.

SUPPLIES

7¾"w x 9⅝"h x 4⅞"d gift bag
Acrylic paints — red, light ivory, flesh, and black
Liquitex® Texture Gel Light Modeling Paste
Antiquing medium or burnt umber acrylic paint
Paintbrushes
Palette knife
Clear acrylic spray sealer
Trims — fabrics, button, and raffia
General Supplies — toothbrush, tracing paper, graphite paper, and a hot glue gun and glue sticks

INSTRUCTIONS

1. For hat, paint top 2¾" of bag red; paint remaining bag light ivory.
2. Trace Santa Bag Face pattern (pg. 8) onto tracing paper. Place graphite paper, coated side down, on bag. Place traced pattern on top of graphite paper. Draw over traced pattern.
3. Paint face.
4. Texturize hat trim and mustache using Modeling Paste.
5. Antique bag.
6. Spatter paint bag with light ivory acrylic paint.
7. Spray bag with acrylic sealer.
8. Glue fabric patches and button to Santa. Tie raffia shoelace-style bow around handle.

FABRIC HEARTS GIFT BAG

Photo, pg. 16

Please read General Instructions, pg. 1.

SUPPLIES

8"w x 10½"h x 4½"d gift bag
Paper-backed fusible web
Fabrics
Black felt-tip permanent pen
Trims — buttons, raffia, and a jingle bell
General Supplies — hot glue gun and glue sticks

INSTRUCTIONS

1. Trace Medium Heart pattern (pg. 24) desired number of times onto paper-backing side of fusible web. Fuse web to wrong side of fabrics; cut along drawn lines. Fuse hearts to bag.
2. Use permanent pen to add details between hearts.
3. Add trims to bag as follows:
   Glue buttons to bag front.
   Tie raffia shoelace-style bows around handle.
   Glue jingle bell to bow.

GINGERBREAD SNOWMAN GIFT BAG

Photo, pg. 16

Please read General Instructions, pg. 1.

SUPPLIES

8"w x 10½"h x 4½"d gift bag
Heavyweight brown paper bag
Acrylic paints — red, light ivory, black, and orange
Antiquing medium or burnt umber acrylic paint
White dimensional paint
Paintbrushes
Clear acrylic spray sealer
Trims — raffia, buttons, fabrics, and a jingle bell
General Supplies — toothbrush, tracing paper, graphite paper, scissors, craft glue, and a hot glue gun and glue sticks

INSTRUCTIONS

1. Transfer and cut out one Gingerbread Snowman piece (pg. 12) from brown paper bag.
2. Paint Gingerbread Snowman piece.
3. Antique Gingerbread Snowman piece.
4. Paint front of bag red.
5. Use craft glue to glue Gingerbread Snowman piece to bag.
6. Spatter paint bag with light ivory acrylic paint.
7. Spray bag with acrylic sealer.
8. Apply white dimensional paint for trim; allow to dry.
9. Add trims to bag as follows:
    Glue fabric quick-knot bow and jingle bell to Gingerbread Snowman.
    Glue raffia shoelace-style bows and button to handle.
    Glue fabric patches and buttons to bag.

GINGERBREAD BOY GIFT BAG

Photo, front cover

Please read General Instructions, pg. 1.

SUPPLIES

8"w x 10½"h x 4½"d gift bag
Heavyweight brown paper bag
Acrylic paints — light brown, light ivory, red, and black
White dimensional paint
Paintbrushes
Black fine-point permanent pen
Paper-backed fusible web
Clear acrylic spray sealer
Trims — buttons, raffia, fabrics, and a jingle bell
General Supplies — toothbrush, tracing paper, graphite paper, scissors, craft glue, and a hot glue gun and glue sticks

INSTRUCTIONS

1. Transfer and cut out one Gingerbread Boy piece (pg. 11) from brown paper bag.
2. Follow Steps 2-6 of Gingerbread Boy Ornament (pg. 2) to complete Gingerbread Boy.
3. Fuse fusible web to wrong side of fabrics. Cut background, borders, and corner squares. Fuse fabric pieces to bag.
4. Use craft glue to glue Gingerbread Boy to bag.
5. Add trims to bag as follows:
    Glue buttons to bag front.
    Glue raffia shoelace-style bows and button to handle.
    Glue fabric quick-knot bow and jingle bell to Gingerbread Boy.

Angel Stocking Body

Angel Stocking Wings

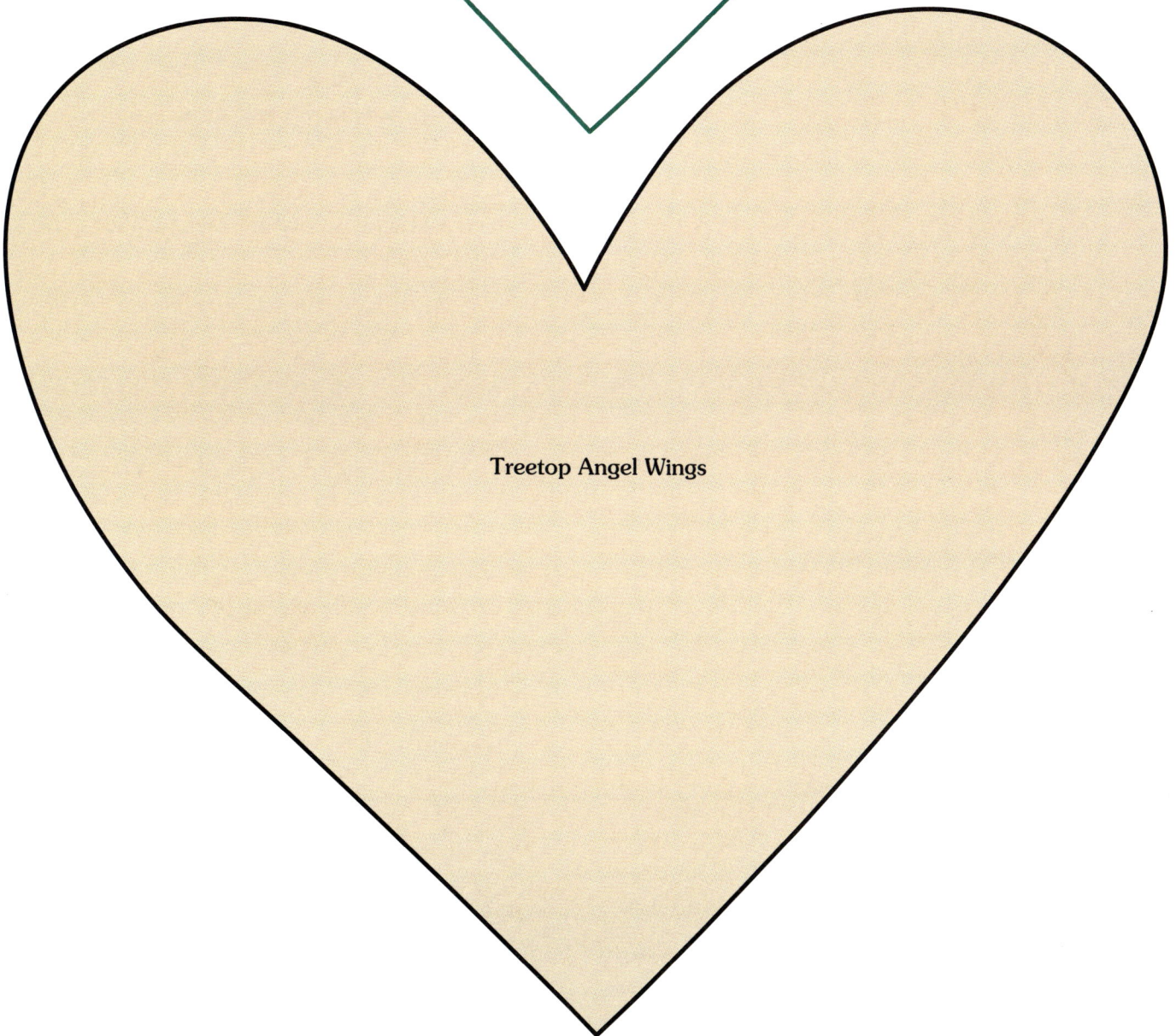

Treetop Angel Wings

● ● ● ● ● ● ● ● ● ● ● ● ● ● ● ● ● ● ●

GINGERBREAD BOY GIFT TAG
Photo, pg. 16

Please read General Instructions, pg. 1.

SUPPLIES
  7³/₄"w x 9⁵/₈"h x 4⁷/₈"d gift bag
  Heavyweight brown paper bag
  Acrylic paints — light brown, light ivory, red, and black
  Paintbrushes
  White dimensional paint
  Black fine-point permanent pen
  Polyester fiberfill
  Clear acrylic spray sealer
  ¹/₈" hole punch
  Trims — fabric, jingle bell, and raffia
  General Supplies — toothbrush, tracing paper, graphite
    paper, scissors, and a hot glue gun and glue sticks

INSTRUCTIONS
1. Follow Steps 1-7 of Gingerbread Boy Ornament (pg. 2) to make Gingerbread Boy.
2. Punch a hole through top of head.
3. Glue fabric quick-knot bow and jingle bell to Gingerbread Boy.
4. Tie raffia shoelace-style bow through hole to attach tag to gift bag handle.

● ● ● ● ● ● ● ● ● ● ● ● ● ● ● ● ● ● ●

GIFT TAGS
Photos, front cover and pg. 16

Please read General Instructions, pg. 1.

SUPPLIES
  Heavyweight paper
  Heavyweight brown paper bag
  Paintbrushes
  ¹/₈" hole punch
  Decorative-edge scissors
  Trims — fabrics, raffia, and buttons
  General Supplies — craft glue and a hot glue gun and
    glue sticks

For Feather Tree tag, you will also need:
  Acrylic paints — green, light ivory, and brown
  Tracing paper
  Graphite paper
  Paintbrushes
  Toothbrush

For Stocking tag, you will also need:
  Acrylic paints — red and light ivory
  Tracing paper
  Graphite paper
  Paintbrushes
  Toothbrush

For Fabric Patch tag, you will also need:
  Black fine-point permanent pen

For Fabric Heart tag, you will also need:
  Paper-backed fusible web

INSTRUCTIONS
1. **For Feather Tree gift tag,** trace Feather Tree Gift Tag pattern (pg. 26) onto tracing paper. Place graphite paper, coated side down, on brown paper bag. Place traced pattern on top of graphite paper. Draw over limb portion of traced pattern. Use base portion of pattern to cut a small fabric patch. Paint trunk and limbs. Spatter paint brown paper bag with light ivory acrylic paint. Use craft glue to glue base to brown paper bag below limbs. Glue raffia shoelace-style bow to tag.
2. **For Stocking gift tag**, trace Stocking Gift Tag pattern (pg. 26) onto tracing paper. Place graphite paper, coated side down, on brown paper bag. Place traced pattern on top of graphite paper. Draw over traced pattern. Paint stocking. Spatter paint brown paper bag with light ivory acrylic paint. Hot glue fabric patches to stocking. Glue raffia shoelace-style bow to tag.
3. **For Fabric Patch gift tag**, hot glue fabric patches to brown paper bag. Write name with permanent pen.
4. **For Fabric Heart gift tag**, trace Medium Heart pattern (pg. 24) onto paper-backing side of fusible web. Fuse web to wrong side of fabric; cut along drawn line. Fuse heart to brown paper bag.
5. For each tag, cut a 3" square of heavyweight paper. Use decorative-edge scissors to cut brown paper bag slightly smaller than heavyweight paper. Use craft glue to glue brown paper bag to tag.
6. Hot glue buttons to tag.
7. Punch a hole in corner of tag. Tie raffia shoelace-style bow through hole.

WRAPPING PAPER

Photos, front cover and pg. 16

Please read General Instructions, pg. 1.

SUPPLIES

Brown kraft paper
Compressed craft sponges
Fine-point permanent pen
Trims — buttons
General Supplies — toothbrush, tracing paper, paper
  plate, paper towels, scissors, and a hot glue gun and
  glue sticks

For Gingerbread Boy paper, you will also need:
Acrylic paints — dark brown, light ivory, red, and black
Paintbrushes
Fabrics

For Holly paper, you will also need:
Acrylic paints — green, red, and light ivory
Fabrics

For Hearts and Stars paper, you will also need:
Acrylic paints — red, gold, and light ivory

INSTRUCTIONS

1. Cut a piece of kraft paper large enough to wrap package.
2. **For Gingerbread Boy paper,** sponge paint paper desired number of times using Gingerbread Boy pattern (pg. 24). Add icing, eyes, buttons, and bows with acrylic paints.
3. **For Holly paper,** sponge paint paper desired number of times using Holly pattern (pg. 24). Add berries with acrylic paint and the eraser end of a pencil.
4. **For Hearts and Stars paper,** sponge paint paper desired number of times using Small Heart and Star patterns (pg. 24).
5. Spatter paint wrapping paper with light ivory acrylic paint.
6. **For Gingerbread Boy and Holly paper,** glue fabric patches to wrapping paper.
7. Glue buttons to wrapping paper.

NOTE CARDS

Photos, front cover and pg. 6

Please read General Instructions, pg. 1.

SUPPLIES

Heavyweight paper
Heavyweight brown paper bag
Decorative-edge scissors
Trims — fabrics and buttons
General Supplies — craft glue and a hot glue gun and
  glue sticks

For Santa card, you will also need:
Acrylic paints — red, light ivory, flesh, and black
Paintbrushes
General Supplies — toothbrush, tracing paper, and
  graphite paper

For Tree card, you will also need:
Acrylic paints — green and light ivory
Paintbrushes
Trims — jingle bell and cinnamon stick
General Supplies — toothbrush, tracing paper, and
  graphite paper

For Candy Cane card, you will also need:
Acrylic paints — red, green, and light ivory
Paintbrushes
General Supplies — toothbrush, tracing paper, and
  graphite paper

For Holly and Heart cards, you will also need:
Paper-backed fusible web

INSTRUCTIONS

1. For each note card, cut a 10" x 7" piece of heavyweight paper; fold in half. Using decorative-edge scissors, cut a piece of brown paper bag slightly smaller than front of note card.
2. **For Santa, Tree, and Candy Cane cards,** trace pattern (pg. 24 or 26) onto tracing paper. Place graphite paper, coated side down, on brown paper bag. Place traced pattern on top of graphite paper. Draw over traced pattern. Paint design. Spatter paint brown paper bag with light ivory acrylic paint. Hot glue fabric quick-knot bows, fabric patches, buttons, cinnamon stick, and/or jingle bells to front of cards.
3. **For Holly and Heart cards,** trace pattern (pg. 24) onto paper-backing side of fusible web. Fuse web to wrong side of fabrics; cut along drawn lines. Fuse shapes to front of card. Hot glue buttons to card.
4. Use craft glue to glue brown paper bag to front of card.

Treetop Angel Body

23

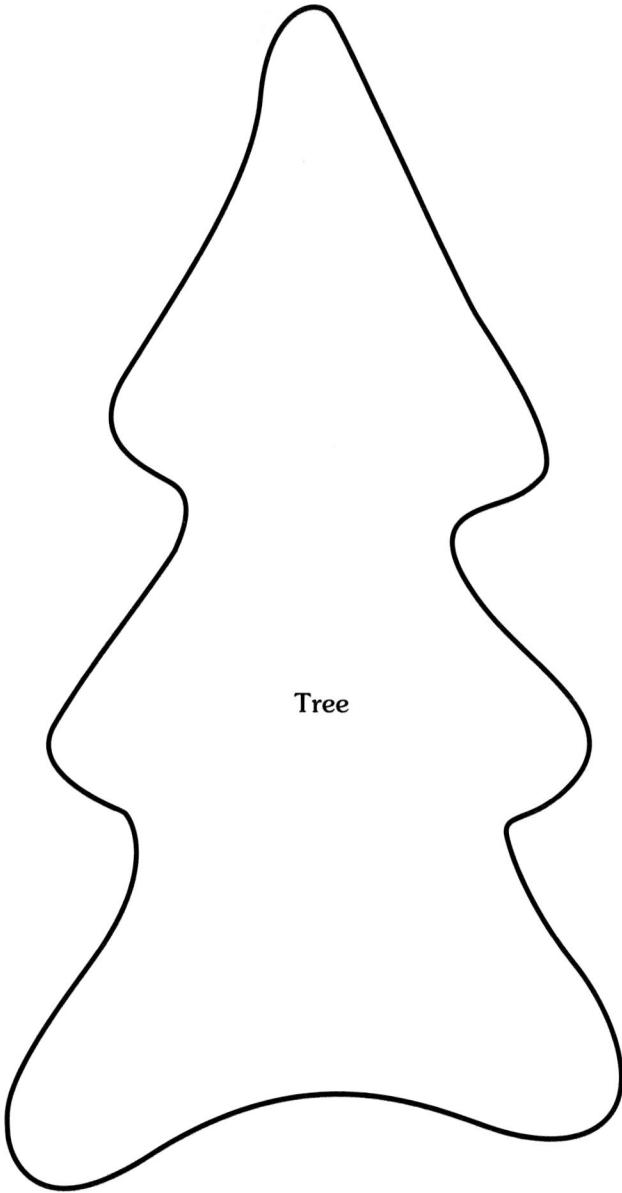

Tree

Star

Medium Heart

Holly

Small Heart

Gingerbread Boy

Reindeer Bag Face

Reindeer Bag Antler

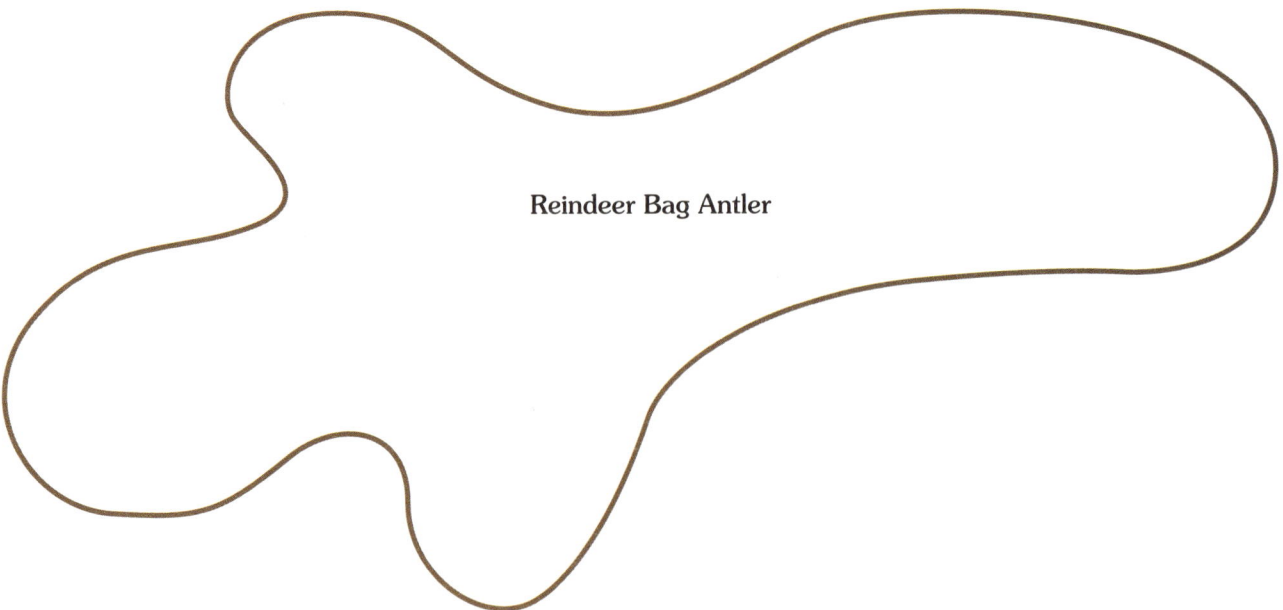

Stocking Gift Tag

Candy Cane Note Card

Feather Tree Gift Tag

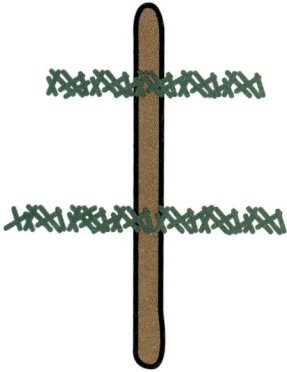

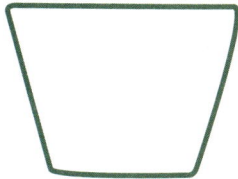

Santa Note Card

26

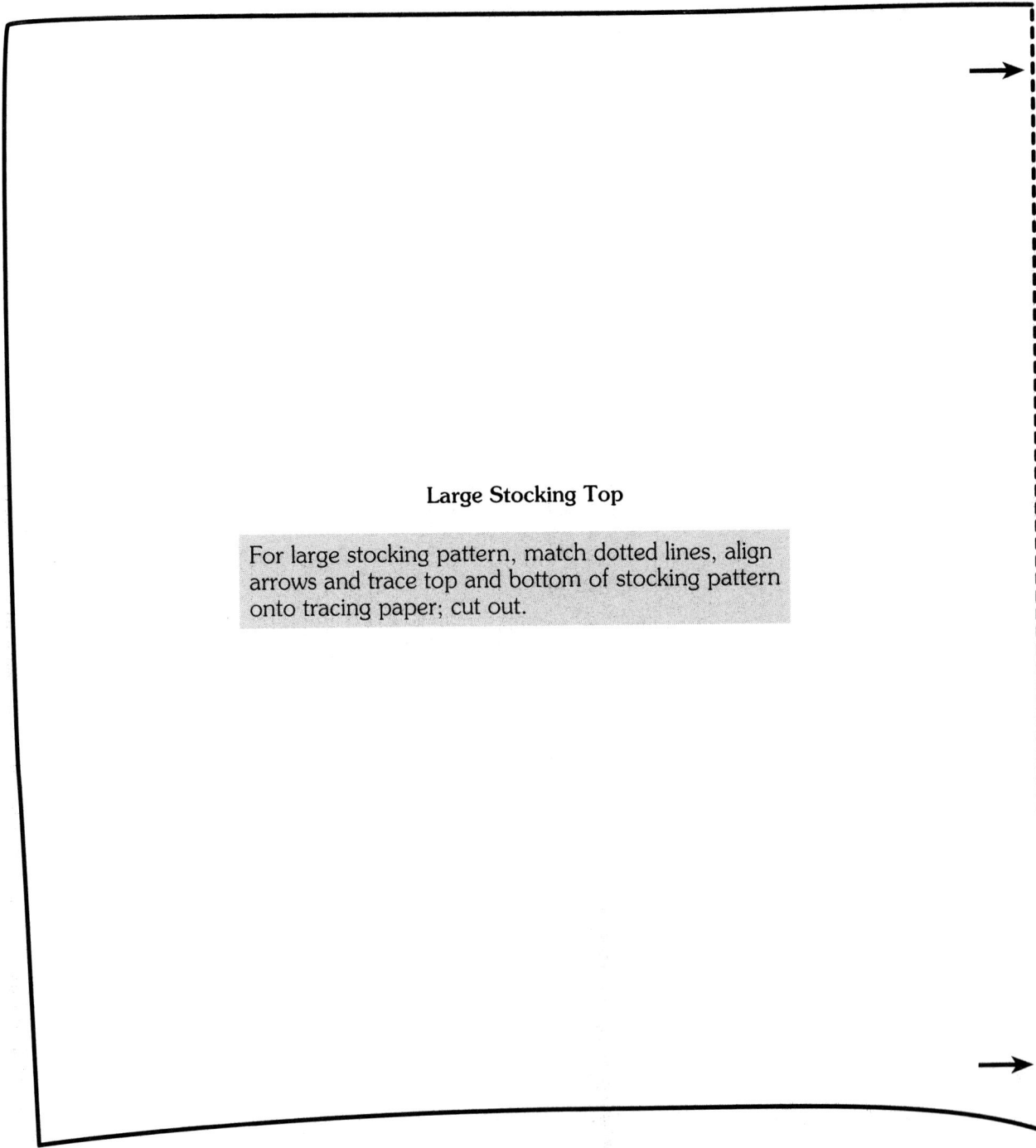

Large Stocking Top

For large stocking pattern, match dotted lines, align arrows and trace top and bottom of stocking pattern onto tracing paper; cut out.

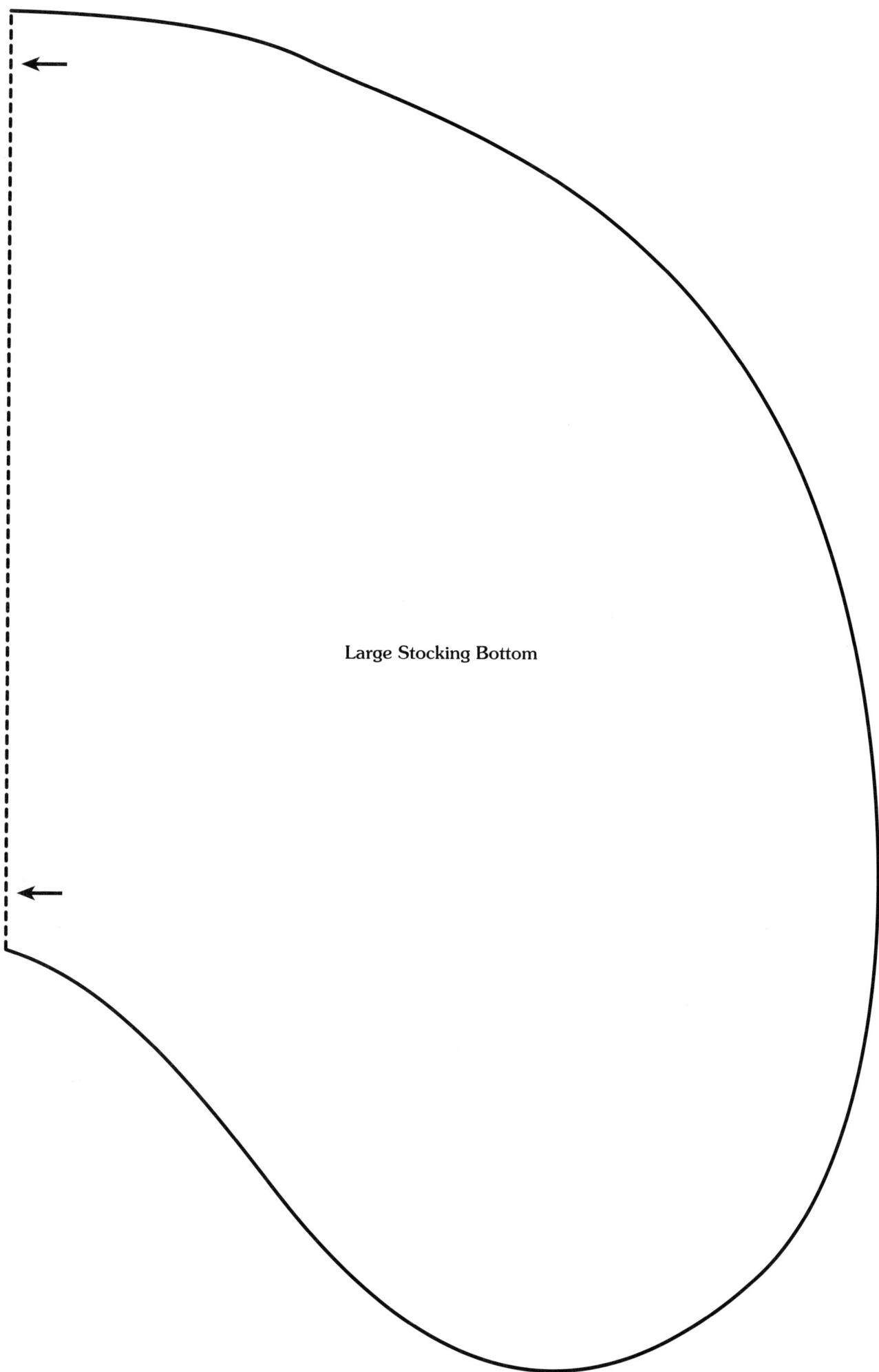

Large Stocking Bottom

Medium Stocking

Small Stocking

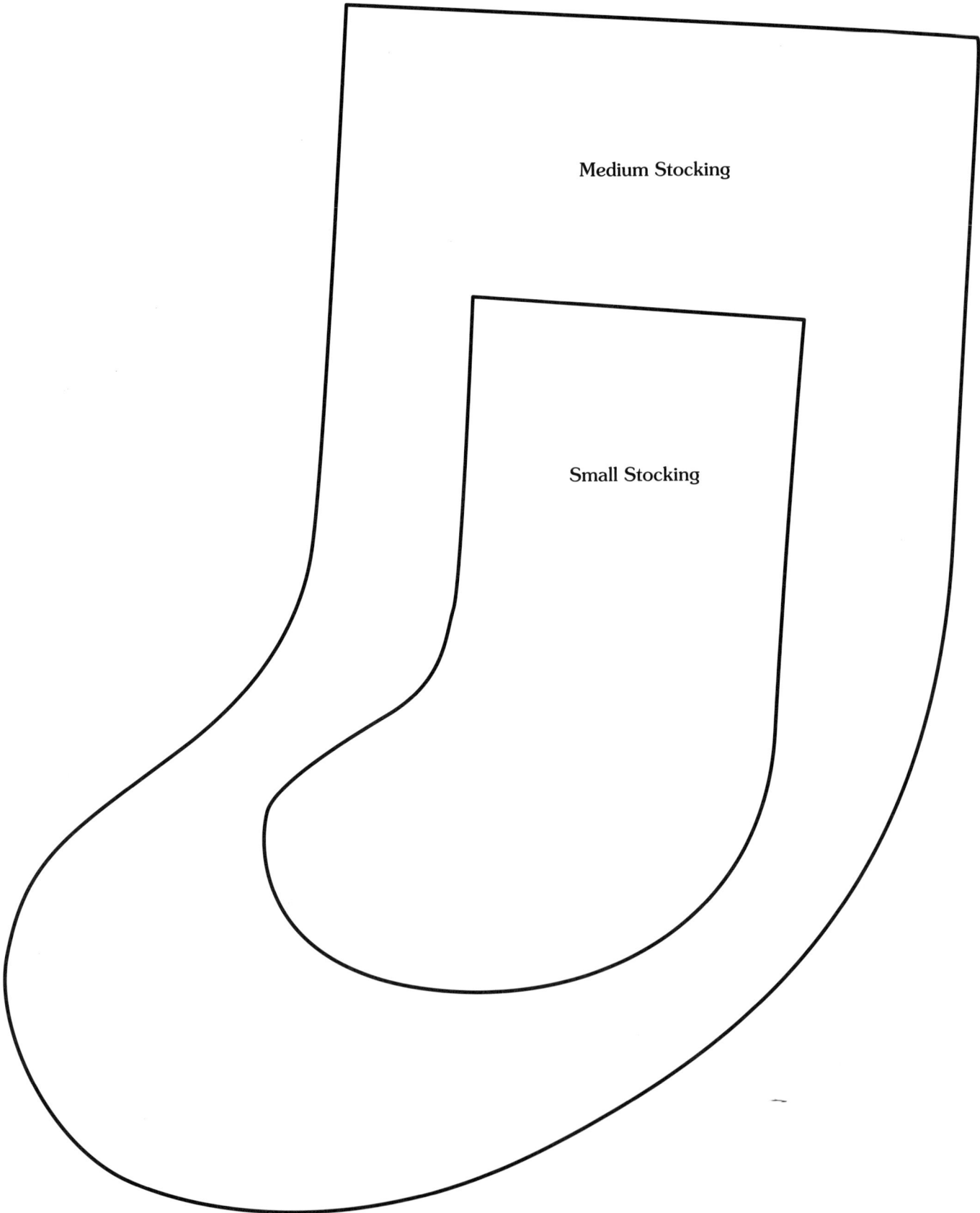